A MULTI-SENSORY READING METHODOLOGY

The Fantastic Syllable Division Book

Jeanne M. Liuzzo
Director of Instruction

Bronwyn Hain, Training Coordinator

Institute for Multi-Sensory Education
24800 Denso Drive, Ste. 202
Southfield, Michigan 48033
Phone 800-646-9788 · Fax 248-735-2927

E-mail: imse@orton-gillingham.com   Web: www.imse.com

institute for
multi-sensory
education

0519-01

Table of Contents

Table of Contents (cont.)

Note: When sentences are included, students can have practice reading the words in sentences. Teachers can also use the words and sentences as additional dictation if desired.

Decoding Guide

How to Decode
1. Find the first two vowels (vowel sounds), underline them and label with a V.
2. Draw a line (bridge) connecting the bottom of the two V's ex. V____V.
3. Underline and label the consonant(s) above the bridge with a C ex. VCCV.
4. Find pattern and divide word into syllables.
5. Label each syllable type (Cl, O, ME, VT, BR, DT, C-LE).
6. Read each syllable, then blend into word.
7. Check for comprehension or refer to dictionary for meaning.

How to Decode Three or More Syllables
1. Find the first two vowels (vowel sounds), underline them and label with a V.
2. Draw a line (bridge) connecting the bottom of the two V's, ex. V____V.
3. Label the letter(s) above the bridge with a C, ex. VCCV.
4. Find pattern and divide word into syllables.
5. Check to see if there is another vowel that is not an "e" at the end of a word.
6. If so, cover up the letters to the 2nd labeled vowel and find the next vowel and label with a V.

7. With off hand still covering up to the 2nd labeled vowel, draw a bridge connecting the bottom of the two vowels.
8. Label the consonant(s) above the bridge with a C, ex. VCCV.
9. Find pattern and divide word into syllables.
10. Label each syllable type (Cl, O, ME, VT, BR, DT, C-LE).
11. Read each syllable then put together.
12. Check for comprehension or refer to dictionary for meaning.

VC/CV
**Compound Words with Closed (Cl) &
Closed (Cl) Syllables**

The vowel consonant/consonant vowel is the first syllable pattern to be introduced in conjunction with the open and closed syllable type. Using compound words can be a good way to bridge from monosyllabic words to multisyllabic words.

Example:

	Decode:		Encode:
	Cl	Cl	
	b a̲ t̲h̲	t u̲ b	b a̲ t̲h̲ t u̲ b
	v c	c v	

sunset

Batman

catfish

upset

bobcat

cannot

dishpan

cancan

sunlit

upshot

bathtub

bedbug

suntan

catnip

pigpen

inlet

sunfish

cashbox

Please note:

If there are more than two consonants, look for known digraphs. Underline and label them as one consonant.

Compound Words with Closed Syllables

Have students practice reading sentences for automaticity. These can also be used for dictation.

1. The sunset is dim.
2. The man got a cod and a catfish.
3. The dishpan is in the bathtub.
4. The cat upset the catfish.
5. Batman set the cashbox on the ship.
6. The ship hit the inlet.
7. The pigpen has mud.
8. The bedbug bit the dog.
9. The bobcat ran.
10. The fish was a sunfish.

VC/CV
Two Syllable Words with Closed (Cl)
& Open (O) Syllables

lasso	motto	muffin
combat	candid	fossil
rustic	napkin	rabbit
wombat	picnic	fabric
hiccup	tablet	goblin
tennis	witness	quintet*
possum	cactus	acquit*
Jello	tempo	
hello	hippo	
gumbo	combo	
jumbo	jumbo	
limbo	ditto	
alto	goddess	
mascot	expel	
confess	submit	
banjo	gusto	
gossip	admit	

Please note:

*Remind students to label qu as one consonant unit.

Two Syllable VC/CV Sentences
with Closed and Open Syllables

1. Dennis is a gossip and will not stop.
2. The shot upset the bobcat.
3. Melvin put the muffin in the picnic basket.
4. Maxwell will win at tennis.
5. Do not dip the napkin in the muffin mix.
6. Give the rabbit a bit of catnip.
7. The hubbub of the bash upset the lad.
8. The fabric of the dress is velvet.
9. The goblin ran pass the wombat.
10. Will Batman combat the thug?
11. The chap does not wish to go to the rustic hamlet.
12. The mascot of the school is a possum.
13. Did the bandit confess to the cop?
14. Will Elvis commit to wed the lass at sunset?
15. The school will expel the bad lad.
16. Tom will submit the bill.
17. The quintet will sing at the shop.
18. Did you picnic at sunset?

Two Syllable VC/CV Sentences
with Closed and Open Syllables

Have students practice reading sentences for
automaticity. These can also be used for dictation.

19. The pot of gumbo is hot.

20. The tempo of the banjo is madcap.

21. Dennis will sip on the gumbo with gusto.

22. Otto will hum to the tempo of the banjo.

23. The motto of the mascot is, "Rev up the tempo!"

24. Lasso the pig before it can run from the pigpen!

25. A fat hippo cannot fit in a tub.

26. Jim cannot commit to a job.

27. "I will not gossip," said Edwin. "Ditto!" said Dennis.

28. Do not tell me that mumbo jumbo.

6   © 2019 IMSE

V/CV
Two Syllable Words with Closed (Cl) & Open (O) Syllables

The second pattern that is introduced is vowel/consonant vowel. This pattern can be introduced when vc/cv is taught or independently.

Example:

	Decode:	Encode:
	O | Cl	
	t <u>o</u> <u>p</u> a z	<u>t</u> <u>o</u> <u>p</u> <u>a</u> <u>z</u>
	<u>v</u>|<u>c</u> v	

lotus	token	credo
mason	halo	polo
latex	bogus	tripod
unit	focus	judo
ego	open	
polo	basic	
topaz	even	
veto	basin	
totem	omen	
cupid	hogan	
pagan	raven	
hobo	thesis	
item	humid	
bonus	tulip	
robot	tunic	

Please note:

When students are faced with the pattern VCV, they should always try V/CV first and pronounce word. If they do not recognize the word, try VC/V for pronounciation.

(See page 31)

Two Syllable V/CV Sentences
with Closed and Open Syllables

Have students practice reading sentences for automaticity. These can also be used for dictation.

1. Otis will not picnic if it is humid.
2. The math test had no basic problems.
3. At judo class, the student was silent.
4. The math unit had complex problems.
5. Can a robot express that it is sad?
6. A veto can put an end to a bill.
7. A tulip has a smell.
8. The man will dress in a tunic when it is humid.
9. The hobo has a plan for the problem.
10. The dog will combat the robot.
11. Polo is not as fun as tennis.
12. The fish can swim in the basin.
13. A judo student must commit.
14. Did you put the gizmo on the tripod?

Initial Blends
"r" blends

Example:

Decode:	Encode:
Cl | O	
f r e s|c o	fr e s c o
v c|c v	

pilgrim	crimson	Alfred
gremlin	problem	Trenton
kindred	hundred	griskin
trumpet	trodden	spectrum
Crisco	tantrum	ramstram
trellis	entrap	huntress
presto	humdrum	lustrum
grommet	trespass	
grotto	address	
fresco	empress	
impress	anthrax	
mattress	frantic	
traffic	distress	
culprit	griffin	

Please note:

After the first two vowels are underlined and labeled, look for consonants. If there are more than two, look for known digraphs or blends to be labeled as one consonant. Beginning R Blends and L Blends are the most common.

Two Syllable Sentences with Initial R Blends

1. The pilgrim had the address.

2. The frantic huntress has a problem.

3. The trumpet fell on the mattress.

4. I will impress Alfred.

5. Trenton got a ticket in the traffic.

6. We were in a bad traffic jam.

7. Did you tell them the address?

8. The hippo did impress Pam.

Initial Blends
"l" blends

emblem

classic

splendid

glutton

influx

plastid

plummet

slipslop

flimflam

plastic

flotsam

plastron

clampet

slignit

complex

clipclop

flipflop

Please note:

After the first two vowels are underlined and labeled, look for consonants. If there are more than two, look for known digraphs or blends to be labeled as one consonant. Beginning R Blends and L Blends are the most common.

Two Syllable Sentences with Initial L Blends

1. The trellis is plastic.
2. Do not entrap the splendid frog.
3. The classic trumpet is humdrum.
4. The emblem is on the flag.
5. The problem was complex.
6. In class we had to do complex problems.
7. The plastic box fell in the bathtub.
8. He had a classic trumpet.

Initial Blends
"s" blends

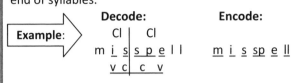

smitten

instep

instill

misspell

skillet

scandal

skeptic

stucco

snapshot

Sentences

1. The cat was smitten with the catnip.
2. I will misspell it.
3. I had the egg on the skillet.
4. Do not be a skeptic.
5. The man had a snapshot of the dog.

Final Blends

"-st" blends

enlist	adjust
attest	consist
tempest	dentist
contest	infest
invest	mistrust
insult	entrust
unrest	contrast
disgust	Baptist
distrust	bombast

Sentences

1. Did you enlist?
2. If you gossip, I will distrust you.
3. The dentist is not a lot of fun.
4. The bedbug will infest the nest.
5. Did you win the contest?

© 2019 IMSE

Final Blends

"-nt blends"

Consonant blends are made up of two to three graphemes in which all the consonant phonemes are heard. Consonant blends occur at the beginning or end of syllables.

Example:

Decode:	Encode:
cl | cl	
s o l v e n t	s o l v e nt
v c | c v	

intent	advent
indent	solvent
pigment	vestment
distant	indignant
segment	fragment
pendent	comment
pendant	consist
convent	content
figment	absent
instant	invent

Sentences

1. Did you comment on the test?
2. Will you invent a new scandal?
3. The man will be absent from the job.
4. The instant Jello will impress me.
5. The nun is in the convent.

Final Blends

"-pt" & "-ct" blends

Consonant blends are made up of two to three graphemes in which all the consonant phonemes are heard. Consonant blends occur at the beginning or end of syllables.

Example:

	Decode:	Encode:
	Cl | Cl	
	s u b|t r a c t	s u b tr a ct
	v c | c v	

disrupt	district	inject
windswept	conduct	object
addict	inspect	expect
intact	convict	intellect
contact	contract	tactless
impact	compact	indirect
insect	inflict	
aspect	instruct	
collect	constrict	
induct	connect	
infect	inflect	
suspect	construct	
prospect	obstruct	
contact	subtract	
conflict	subject	

Two Syllable Sentences with Final -pt and -ct Blends

Have students practice reading sentences for automaticity. These can also be used for dictation.

1. The insect bit me on the leg.
2. A conflict is a problem.
3. Did you subtract or add?
4. The district will send a bus.
5. The man will need to inject the shot into the ill dog.

Final Blends
Other Endings

> Consonant blends are made up of two to three graphemes in which all the consonant phonemes are heard. Consonant blends occur at the beginning or end of syllables.
>
> | | **Decode:** | **Encode:** |
> |---|---|---|
> | Example: | Cl \| Cl | |
> | | i n \| s u l t | i n s u lt |
> | | v c \| c v | |

addend	intend
Finland	insult
distend	twitted
standstill	context
suspend	muskrat
command	contend
windmill	handcuff
pumpkin	expand
numskull	expend
commend	

Sentences

1. In Finland, the man will speak Finnish.
2. The muskrat was in the pond.
3. Do not suspend the lad.
4. Did you take a snapshot of the pumpkin.
5. The contest was at a standstill.

Two Syllable Words

pilgrim	concoct
dentist	infect
Crisco	contact
trellis	prospect
gremlin	distract
fresco	classic
bombast	plastic
emblem	frantic
problem	skeptic
obstruct	handcuff
abstract	insect
subtract	impact
suspect	
addict	

Two Syllable Words

district	nostril
inflict	implant
contest	misstep
consult	imprint
conquest	nonstop
figment	distress
pigment	misprint
segment	misspell
transit	slipslop
mollusk	standstill
Alfred	handgrip
empress	insult
address	engulf
impress	suspend
instill	trumpet

Two Syllable Words

disgust   fragment

plummet   entrust

tantrum   gromwell

entrust

disrupt

mistrust

dandruff

distrust

instep

comment

consist

crimson

consent

absent

kindred

Two Syllable with Closed and
Open Sentence Review Including C-Blends

Have students practice reading sentences for automaticity. These can also be used for dictation.

1. Oshkosh is in Wisconsin.
2. Chad can fill the ad with candid info.
3. The goddess will enchant the goblin.
4. It will be fantastic to swim with a dolphin!
5. Beth will express her love at sunset.
6. The culprit was the bandit at the picnic.
7. Will the pilgrim get on the ship?
8. The math problem is complex.
9. Do not let an insect run up your nostril.
10. When Dustin has a tantrum there is a problem.
11. The mastiff dug up a hundred fossils.
12. Melvin has a dandruff problem.
13. The spectrum of eclectic objects in the shop is big.
14. In math class, we add and subtract.
15. Put the wet poncho in the bathtub.
16. Edwin will entrust Seth to help him nab the culprit.

Three Syllable Words
with and without blends

Always find the first two vowels and divide first two syllables. If there is another vowel in the word that is not an "e" at the end, continue to divide word.

Example: →

Decode:

Cl	Cl	Cl
A t	l a	n t i c

v c | c v | c c v

Encode:

A t l a n t i c

Atlantic	incumbent	diplomat
fantastic	malcontent	mandolin
hobgoblin	alfresco	abdomen
adjustment	contralto	succulent
insistent	Wisconsin	piccolo
intellect	palmetto	succotash
commitment	eclectic	
bombastic	Algonquin	
lemniscus	appendix	
encompass	espresso	
agnostic	commandment	
prognostic	enchantress	
intrinsic	acrobat	
encampment	octopus	
disconnect	daffodil	

Please note:

Remember if there are more than two consonants, look for known digraphs or blends.

Three Syllable with Closed and Open Sentences

Have students practice reading sentences for automaticity. These can also be used for dictation.

1. Maxwell is fantastic at tennis and badminton.
2. We will fish for catfish in the Atlantic.
3. A mantis hid in the palmetto.
4. Elvis got a gizmo at the eclectic shop.
5. Bob cannot commit to go to Wisconsin .
6. The Algonquin people do not live by the Atlantic.
7. Willis got his banjo in Wisconsin.
8. We can picnic alfresco if the sun is out.
9. Maxwell has an intrinsic gift at tennis.
10. I wish to sip a cup of hot espresso with a dab of nutmeg.
11. Pam is the one contralto in the quintet.
12. The glasses must have an adjustment to fit.
13. Command Dustin to stop his tantrum.
14. A commitment must last.
15. The acrobat can bend and jump.
16. Can I fish for an octopus in the Atlantic?
17. Which is the best gift: a tulip or a daffodil?
18. Can the diplomat fix the problem?
19. David will strum the mandolin.
20. The music student has a piccolo and a mandolin.
21. Succotash is best when fresh and hot.

Decoding Words with ng/nk

Have students practice circling the ng/nk unit that ends a syllable. Then have them split the word and read.

Example:

	Decode:	**Encode:**
	r(ing)/ let	r ing l e t

ringlet	mustang	inkling
longhand	chipmunk	anklet
songfest	trinket	bankrupt
kingpin	Franklin	inkwell
hamstring	plankton	databank

Sentences

1. Franklin got the plankton in the lake.
2. The ringlet fell on her face.
3. The mustang will chase the chipmunk.
4. I had an inkling that I would get an anklet.
5. Do not go bankrupt!

Decoding Words with Suffix -ed

landed   spilled   fussed

spelled   pinched   smelled

rushed   jaded   happened

dished   indisposed   relaxed

crushed   famished   adopted

yelled   frustrated   uninhabited

melted   committed

Sentences

1. She landed at the bottom of the step.
2. He spelled it like it should be spelled.
3. The dog was famished when she came home.
4. The man was frustrated at the cat.
5. The dog smelled so bad, but she still adopted him.

Please note:

The sounds of -ed: If the base word ends in d or t, -ed will say /id/. If the base ends in a voiced sound, -ed will say /d/. If the base ends in an unvoiced sound, -ed will say /t/.

Third Syllable Type:
Magic E (ME) Two Syllable Words

The Magic E jumps over one consonant and empowers the single vowel to shout its own name.

Example:

Decode:

Cl | ME
e x | h a l | e
v c | c v

Encode:

e x h a l e ★★★

contrive	inside	cremate
combine	invite	butane
reptile	escape	elope
dislike	dictate	vacate
trombone	compete	grenade
cascade	dispute	consume
cupcake	insane	concrete
landscape	complete	stampede
bathrobe	pancake	confide
imbibe	extreme	conclude
mistake	compute	invoke
mandate	invade	transcribe
sublime	exhale	exclude
mundane	shipshape	debate
benzene	membrane	cognate
inhale	textile	humane
tadpole	connive	obese
unsafe	ignite	

Magic E (ME)
Three Syllable Words

Example:

Decode: **Encode:**

Cl | Cl | ME

i n | t e s | t a t e   i n t e s t a t e ★★★

v c | c v c | c v

compensate

illustrate

infiltrate

infantile

contemplate

amputate

envelope

antelope

intestate

confiscate

obsolete

incubate

pantomime

accolade

Third Syllable Type: Magic E (ME) Sentences

Have students practice reading sentences for automaticity. These can also be used for dictation.

1. Will the men invade the combat zone?
2. Melvin must not fixate on his dandruff problem.
3. I will vacate my home if a snake gets inside!
4. The soft bathrobe is made of velvet.
5. Pete fell off his bike and hit the concrete.
6. We will hike to the cascade at the top of the slope.
7. The flat landscape will make the bike ride less difficult.
8. Edwin will not confide in Dennis.
9. Maxwell must not assume that he will win the tennis game.
10. Jake and Jane hope to elope and save the cost of a wedding.
11. The impact of the volcano was extreme.
12. Is a trumpet as big as a trombone?
13. Steve will transcribe the note if you dictate it to him.

Third Syllable Type: Magic E (ME) Sentences

Have students practice reading sentences for automaticity. These can also be used for dictation.

14. It is rude to exclude Dale from the club.

15. Jan will write and Jane will illustrate.

16. Antelope like to run in the sand.

17. Calculate the tax on the sale of the home.

18. Mom had to confiscate Fido's stash of bones.

19. Put the note in and envelope.

20. Is a landline phone obsolete?

21. Edwin must contemplate the risks when he confides in Dennis.

22. The sub gave the class a math ditto to complete.

3rd Syllable Pattern:
VC/V

This pattern is the second choice when faced with a vowel consonant vowel pattern. It is introduced separately from the pattern V/CV.

Example:

	Decode:	Encode:
	Cl | Cl	
	r a<u> d</u>|i s h	r <u>a</u> d <u>i</u> <u>sh</u>
	v c | v	

cabin

comic

credit

critic

vivid

denim

panic

radish

project

relic

polish

ravish

colic

seven

rivet

lavish

rapid

livid

static

timid

Spanish

trivet

tepid

tonic

comet

linen

menu

British

epic

finish

blemish

Latin

limit

frolic

vomit

punish

fixate

Please note:

All words on this page are **pattern #3** and are to be divided after the consonant. When students are faced with the pattern vcv, they should always try v/cv first and pronounce word. If it does not sound correct try vc/v for pronunciation. If they still do not know the word, look it up in the dictionary.

Three Syllable Words with Syllable Pattern:

VC/V

This pattern is the second choice when faced with a vowel consonant vowel pattern. It is introduced separately from the pattern V/CV.

Example: →

Decode:	Encode:
Cl Cl	
r a d i s h	r a d i sh
v c v	

volcano

maximum

pimento

difficult

stiletto

reprimand

sentiment

continent

complement

confident

optimist

detriment

pessimist

Please note:

All words on this page are **pattern #3** and are to be divided after the consonant. When students are faced with the pattern vcv, they should always try v/cv first and pronounce word. If it does not sound correct try vc/v for pronunciation. If they still do not know the word, look it up in the dictionary.

Third Syllable Pattern: VC/V Sentences

> Have students practice reading sentences for automaticity. These can also be used for dictation.

1. Gumbo is not on the menu.
2. The epic film will win the contest.
3. Robin did not finish the math problem.
4. Pam had a blemish on her skin.
5. Denim is a fabric.
6. The goddess has a lavish dress.
7. Seven kids in the van is the limit.
8. Kevin must polish the trumpet.
9. Will Robin get credit for her test?
10. The dog will frolic in the sand.
11. Kevin did not intend to vomit.
12. Will the comic offend the critic?
13. Kevin ran from the cabin when he had to vomit.
14. The menu is in Spanish.

Have students practice reading sentences for automaticity. These can also be used for dictation.

15. Is ash from a volcano toxic?

16. The van can fit a maximum of seven mastiffs.

17. Do not put pimento in the gumbo.

18. The math problem is not difficult.

19. The boss will reprimand you if you do a bad job.

20. There are seven continents.

21. The critic will not compliment the comic.

22. Maxwell is confident that he will win at tennis.

23. Kevin is an optimist and is confident that
    he will get well.

24. The pessimist is confident that he will not win.

Decoding with Digraph ph

Have students practice reading words with ph. Underline it as one unit.

Example:

photograph

o | o | cl
ph o t o g r a p h
v c v c v

ph o t o gr a ph
~ -- -- ~

elephant

phoneme

photo

photograph

Phillip

prophet

pamphlet

dolphin

Memphis

Sentences

Please note:

Phl and phr are blends. They are not very common, but you could create a card for those blends if needed.

1. Elvis got a banjo in Memphis.
2. The elephant was on the photo.
3. The old photograph was thin.
4. Phillip had a pamphlet on the program.
5. The dolphin can swim fast.

4th Syllable Type: Vowel Team (VT)

VT - "ea"

mealtime	impeach
meanest	beneath
mistreat	repeat
peanut	defeat
peacock	repeal
reason	bequeath
teacup	retreat
meantime	demean
entreat	reveal
peanut	crabmeat
leaflet	appeal
teapot	teapot
inseam	seamstress
squeamish	

4th Syllable Type: Vowel Team (VT) Sentences

Have students practice reading sentences for automaticity. These can also be used for dictation.

1. Congress can impeach the president.
2. Succotash does not appeal to me.
3. The shop is not open, so in the meantime we can plan the meal.
4. Alvin the chipmunk was dreaming of eating pea-nuts.
5. The team had to retreat from the combat zone.
6. Maxwell will defeat his opponent at tennis.
7. Do not clean the teapot with bleach.
8. The seamstress will fix the rip in the fabric.
9. Dean will bequeath his home to his wife.
10. Do not repeat gossip.
11. Will the beast reveal his secret plot to steal the cupcakes?
12. The cat will squeal and hide beneath the bed.
13. Do not demean Dean with insults.

4th Syllable Type: Vowel Team (VT)

VT - "oa"

A Vowel team is two vowels working together to produce the long vowel phoneme, which is the phoneme of the first vowel. Most commonly taught as "when two vowels go walking, the first one does the talking."

Example:

	Decode:	Encode:
	O	VT	
c	o	c	o a	c o c oa
	v	c v	

bemoan

caseload

coastline

inroad

encroach

oakum

oatmeal

peacoat

reload

reproach

soapbox

steamboat

toadstone

unload

cocoa

crossroad

encroachment

Fourth Syllable Type: Vowel Team (VT) Sentences

Have students practice reading sentences for automaticity. These can also be used for dictation.

1. Joan likes to drive by the Atlantic coastline.
2. The coach gave the team hot cocoa with cream.
3. If you approach the toad, it will croak.
4. Help the coach reload the van.
5. Do not encroach upon the foal while it roams.
6. Joan will moan and groan if her caseload is big.
7. The steamboat will chug a load of coal.
8. A roach ran across the dish of oatmeal.
9. Will the toadstone help the men in combat?
10. Mom must reproach Dustin when he has a tantrum.
11. Maxwell will not bemoan a loss at tennis.
12. Jan will moan if you make her put on a peacoat.
13. Joan will help Jane unload the boat.
14. Go to the left when you reach the crossroad.

4th Syllable Type: Vowel Team (VT)

VT - "ai"

A Vowel team is two vowels working together to produce the long vowel phoneme, which is the phoneme of the first vowel. Most commonly taught as "when two vowels go walking, the first one does the talking."

Example:

	Decode:		Encode:
	Cl	VT	
	e x	p l a i n	e x pl ai n
	v c	c v	

mainstream	mailman	sailboat
contain	mislaid	detain
constraint	obtain	refrain
abstain	painful	acclaim
bailiff	proclaim	hangnail
blackmail	reclaim	maintain
bobtail	remain	plaintiff
complain	retain	acquaint
complaint	sustain	
detail	tailcoat	
disdain	tailgate	
email	vainest	
entail	waitress	
explain	coattail	
handrail	railroad	

4th Syllable Type: Vowel Team (VT) Sentences

Have students practice reading sentences for automaticity. These can also be used for dictation.

1. The coach cannot proclaim that the team will win.
2. The plaintiff will refrain from comment.
3. It is not safe to tailgate when you drive.
4. The actress will win acclaim for her role in the film.
5. Dale will not take the train because of the time constraint.
6. Gail will complain if the mailman is late.
7. Jane has disdain for the mailman because he puts her mail in Dave's mailbox.
8. The bailiff had to lead the witness to the stand.
9. Gail bit the hangnail.
10. The frail man cannot maintain a smile.
11. The bailiff will acquaint the witness with the rules.
12. Can Jane obtain the document?
13. Will the plaintiff win the case?

4th Syllable Type: Vowel Team (VT)

VT - "ee"

A Vowel team is two vowels working together to produce the long vowel phoneme, which is the phoneme of the first vowel. Most commonly taught as "when two vowels go walking, the first one does the talking."

Example:

	Decode:		**Encode:**
	Cl | VT		
	e s t e e m		e s t ee m
	v c c v		

discreet

Kathleen

indeed

fifteen

sixteen

coffee

absentee

amputee

chimpanzee

committee

teepee

toffee

canteen

coffeecake

esteem

enlistee

feedback

offscreen

Tennessee

sweepstake

beehive

redeem

between

seventeen

flaxseed

beeline

discreet

jubilee

pedigree

4th Syllable Type: Vowel Team (VT) Sentences

Have students practice reading sentences for automaticity. These can also be used for dictation.

1. Fill the canteen so that you can drink while you hike.
2. When Dustin put his hand inside the beehive, he got stung.
3. I have no esteem for the candidate.
4. Maxwell is indeed a tennis pro.
5. The plaintiff and the defendant do not agree.
6. Alvin made a beeline to the stove.
7. Will weevils eat the crops?
8. The committee will vote on the rule.
9. The chimpanzee likes to eat meat.
10. Joan will mail her vote to Tennessee as an absentee.
11. The grand jubilee will be held in Memphis, Tennessee.
12. The pedigree of the dog will impress the critics.

4th Syllable Type: Vowel Team (VT)

VT - "ay"

Example:

Decode:		Encode:
O VT		
F r i d a y		Fr i d ay
v c v		

subway

essay

Sunday

dismay

Bombay

display

crayfish

crayon

maybe

playtime

mayhem

playmate

relay

okay

Friday

delay

decay

freeway

maypole

hayseed

hayride

dismay

ashtray

mainstay

Fourth Syllable Type: Vowel Team (VT) Sentences

Have students practice reading sentences for automaticity. These can also be used for dictation.

1. At the end of playtime, the children like to drink cocoa.

2. Jay can run fast and may help the team win the relay.

3. When traffic is bad, I hate to drive on the freeway.

4. On Friday, Jay will display his talent when he plays the trombone in public.

5. A crayon can melt in the hot sun.

6. To the coach's dismay, his top team lost the game.

7. The playmates had a blast on the hayride!

8. Your teeth will decay if you do not brush and floss.

9. The student must fix the mistakes on his essay by Friday, or he will fail the class.

10. The crash on the freeway will lead to a long delay.

11. Crayfish inhabit the fresh stream.

12. It will be mayhem on the freeway, so it is best to take the subway.

13. The ashtray stunk, so Kay had to clean it with bleach.

14. When the mudslide came, Jay waited on the side of the road.

15. The weevils ate the mainstay crop.

4th Syllable Type: Vowel Team (VT)

VT - "oe"

> A Vowel team is two vowels working together to produce the long vowel phoneme, which is the phoneme of the first vowel. Most commonly taught as "when two vowels go walking, the first one does the talking."
>
> **Example:** ⟹
>
> | | Decode: | | Encode: |
> |---|---|---|---|
> | | Cl | VT | |
> | | t i p | t o e | t i p t oe |
> | | v c | c v | |

doeskin

roebuck

roscoe

tiptoe

toenail

oboe

pekoe

Sentences

1. Joe can play the oboe, and Jay can play the trombone.
2. Joan likes to paint her toenails pink.
3. The doeskin was soft.
4. The coach must stand on tiptoe to reach the equipment.
5. Pekoe is a fine tea.

5th Syllable Type: Bossy R (BR)

BR - "er"

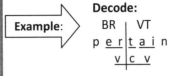

(Also called r-controlled) The "r" controls the vowel and produces an entirely new phoneme.

Example:

Decode:
$$\begin{array}{c|c} \text{BR} & \text{VT} \\ \text{p e} \underline{\text{r}} \, \underline{\text{t}} \, \text{a i} \, \text{n} \\ \underline{\text{v}} & \underline{\text{c}} \quad \text{v} \end{array}$$

Encode:

p e r t ai n

advert	bittersweet	inferno
aftermath	blockbuster	peppermint
Alexander	blunder	imposter
antler	butternut	scatterbrain
blister	cackler	referee
luster	bluster	entertain
prosper	caster	terminate
rafter	cater	exterminate
thermometer	chandler	
culvert	verdict	
otter	hamster	
aftertime	mutter	
administer	lantern	
adverb	perplex	
hermit	vermin	
litter	beaver	
asterisk	expert	
casserole	persist	
canister	verbose	

Please note:

When a word ends with –er, check to see if a base word proceeds it. If so, -er is a suffix and could be circled and a line drawn before it.

example: p r i n t | er

5th Syllable Type: Bossy R (BR)

BR - "er"

(Also called r-controlled) The "r" controls the vowel and produces an entirely new phoneme.

Example:

Decode:
BR | VT
p e̲r̲ | t a̲i̲ n
v | c v

Encode:
p e̲r̲ t a̲i̲ n

chatterbox	hinder
lobster	scamper
berserk	termite
clutter	roster
twitter	vertex
stutter	perplex
cleaner	pervade
perfume	utter
perfect	Amsterdam
cleaver	intersect
plunder	suspender
cloverleaf	interrupt
pamper	
western	
vesper	

Please note:

If affixes have been taught, circle prefix or suffix and draw a line after or before. Students can circle examples:

h u n t (er)   (re) p r i n t (ed)

5th Syllable Type: Bossy R (BR) Sentences

Have students practice reading sentences for automaticity. These can also be used for dictation.

1. The perfume has a strong smell.
2. The silver ring lost its luster, so the preacher had to polish it.
3. Speak up! Do not mutter when you read the verse.
4. Will the complex math problem perplex the student?
5. The hamster likes to run on the wheel.
6. Will the beaver cross the dam?
7. Coach Ernest will post the roster next week.
8. The butler will never complain to the maid.
9. The teacher is a math expert.
10. The athlete will persist despite pain and will cross the finish line.
11. Run fast to escape the inferno!
12. If you interrupt Gertrude when she is speaking, she will scream.
13. Interpret the map to see if the roads intersect.

Have students practice reading sentences for automaticity. These can also be used for dictation.

14. Drink peppermint tea when you do not feel well.

15. Herbert is a scatterbrain and cannot remember if he ate dinner.

16. Ernest will entertain us by playing the oboe.

17. Will the boss terminate the contract?

18. The teacher will administer the exam.

19. Put the thermometer in the container so that it will not shatter if you drop it.

20. Alexander will agree not to pester the butler.

21. Herbert must exterminate the termites.

5th Syllable Type: Bossy R (BR)

BR - "ir"

(Also called r-controlled) The "r" controls the vowel and produces an entirely new phoneme.

Example:

Decode:
$$
\begin{array}{c}
\text{BR} \quad \text{ME} \\
\text{v i r g u l e} \\
\text{v} \quad \text{c} \quad \text{v}
\end{array}
$$

Encode:

v i r g u l e ***

birdbath	twirling
birdseed	undershirt
birthstone	virgate
confirm	virgule
firkin flirted	zircon
hummingbird	respirate
infirm	elixir
jaybird	birthdate
mirthless	Virgo
redshirt	birthday
seabird	skirmish
squirted	aspirate
stirrup	Birmingham
thirteen	aspirin
thunderbird	

5th Syllable Type: Bossy R (BR) Sentences

Have students practice reading sentences for automaticity. These can also be used for dictation.

1. The infirm man was too weak to stand up.
2. Alexander will be thirteen on his next birthday.
3. Does Irving consider Friday the thirteenth a day to be afraid of?
4. Send an email to Irwin to confirm the meeting.
5. A skirmish between the players made the referee end the game.
6. Adding a birthstone to the silver ring will make it a perfect gift.
7. The jay likes to swim in the birdbath.
8. Irwin's birthdate is the day after mine.
9. Will the cat jump up and consume the birdseed?
10. The coach had to redshirt the athlete and develop his skills.
11. The hummingbird will relax in the birdbath.

5th Syllable Type: Bossy R (BR) Sentences

Have students practice reading sentences for automaticity. These can also be used for dictation.

12. Irwin will confirm the time of the meeting so that he is not late.

13. Irving did not stop in Birmingham because he still had to drive a long way.

14. Do you think that the thunderbird will alert us of thunder?

15. If you take the aspirin, you will feel better and can play tennis with Maxwell.

5th Syllable Type: Bossy R (BR)

BR - "ur"

(Also called r-controlled) The "r" controls the vowel and produces an entirely new phoneme.

Example:

Decode:

BR	Cl
t u r	n i p
v	c v

Encode:

t ur n i p

disturb	microburst	curtail
survive	burro	femur
turban	churchgoer	curriculum
blurter	hamburger	furbish
surplus	furnisher	depurate
bulgur	concur	further
murmur	hurdler	curser
burden	incur	suburb
curate	concurrent	turnstile
burgonet	perturb	turpentine
curbside	frankfurter	surrender
overturn	current	hurricane
burlap	disturb	
curler	durum	
burnet	exurb	

5th Syllable Type: Bossy R (BR) Sentences

1. Gertrude will help furnish the den with eclectic objects.
2. Fill the burlap bag with birdseed to feed to the hummingbirds.
3. Westminster is a suburb of Denver.
4. Speak up! If you murmur, you will not win the debate.
5. If you perturb Herbert the butler, he may quit.
6. Use the surplus fabric from the dress to make a skirt.
7. Never jump over the turnstile to the subway!
8. Use turpentine to get a paint stain off of a rug.
9. The combat will go on until one side agrees to surrender.
10. I will order a thick hamburger with crisp bacon, tomato, and peanut butter.
11. Frank likes to grill frankfurters and slather them in fresh tomatoes.
12. You must seek shelter to protect your children from the hurricane.

Syllable Pattern #4
V/V

The last syllable pattern taught is vowel/vowel.

	Decode:	Encode:
Example:	o o c v i | o | l i n v | v | c v	v i o l i n

poet

poem

create

cameo

video

dialect

oasis

violent

diagnose

rodeo

Sentences

1. The poet will create a poem.
2. The actress had a cameo in the skit.
3. The midwest dialect is different than the west coast.
4. I need a vacation to an oasis destination.
5. The rodeo was fun.

Please note:

When a vowel pattern looks like it might be a vowel team, but it is not working together, that is called an unstable digraph. An example is oasis. When two vowels are next to each other, but are never a vowel team, they are called adjacent vowels like in rodeo.

6th Syllable Type: Diphthongs (DT)

DT - "ow"

A diphthong is a gliding vowel. The mouth starts at one point of articulation and ends at another point.

Example:

	Decode:		Encode:
	DT	BR	
	p o w	e r	p ow er
	v	v	

bellflower	downsize
cowboy	downtown
cower	endow
cowhide	however
power	vowel
towel	manpower
downgrade	meow
flower	overpower
Howitzer	sundown
shower	tower
safflower	prowess
powder	
chowder	
download	

6th Syllable Type: Diphthong (DT) Sentences

Have students practice reading sentences for automaticity. These can also be used for dictation.

1. The cowhide belt is brown and white.

2. To whom will the rich pilot endow his plane?

3. Can we download the video onto the computer?

4. Arthur spilled a heap of powder and did not sweep it up.

5. Whenever the man must leave town, he stays in a hotel.

6. Can you make sure that the clam chowder is fresh and hot.

7. The firm had to downsize in order to maintain a profit.

8. Maxwell hopes that his tennis prowess will lead to grand prizes.

9. Melvin takes the bus to go downtown; however, he prefers to ride the subway.

10. The cat gave a timid meow when the mastiff growled.

11. Petals from a safflower will stain fabric.

12. Maxwell's strong serve allows him to overpower his tennis opponents.

6th Syllable Type: Diphthongs (DT)

DT - "ou"

A diphthong is a gliding vowel. The mouth starts at one point of articulation and ends at another point.

Example:

Decode:
DT | ME
o u t l i n e
v c c v

Encode:
ou t l i n e ★★★

badmouth

backout

bailout

burnout

checkout

cofound

compound

countdown

countercomplaint

devout

discount

expound

impound

countess

founder

flounder

outline

roundup

pronoun

outlandish

groundhog

profound

surround

astound

outstanding

roundabout

thundercloud

6th Syllable Type: Diphthong (DT) Sentences

1. Run to the fish shop and get a pound of flounder.
2. The job of a pronoun is to fill in for a noun.
3. When you must compose an essay, write an outline first.
4. Maxwell is a devout tennis fan.
5. The dentist will discount her rate if you cannot afford to pay.
6. The philosopher makes profound statements that prompt her students to think and be wise.
7. The sweet sound of the harp will astound you.
8. Doghouse is a compound noun.
9. Can a groundhog predict the end of winter?
10. The grouch wrote an outstanding essay about the founder of the town.
11. Will the bold actress don an outlandish gown?
12. The scout who spoke in a roundabout manner lost the debate.
13. Coach Kevin did not let the team play outside until the thundercloud went away.

Decoding Practice for igh

highway

nightlight

flashlight

highness

nightmare

twilight

limelight

spotlight

brighten

frighten

Sentences

1. Did you use a flashlight at night?
2. Do not frighten the bat.
3. Can you put a spotlight on the deer?
4. I had a nightmare at twilight.
5. I do not like the limelight.

7th Syllable Type: Consonant -le (C-le)

C-le occurs at the end of a syllable and is represented as a vowel sound. The c-le is circled, dividing the word into two syllables.

Example: ➡

Decode:

Cl | c-le
s i z (z l e)
v

Encode:

s i z zle

muzzle

puzzle

kettle

ample

toddle

ladle

gaggle

tattle

sizzle

tumble

title

griddle

noble

scruple

fiddle

muffle

maple

stifle

coddle

nozzle

twiddle

paddle

gable

bottle

wiggle

middle

pimple

rumble

Please note:

Students must be taught that the "e" at the end is silent but with the consonant +le it is represented as a syllable. Consonant –le should be circled and then a line drawn in front.

7th Syllable Type: Consonant -le (C-le)

C-le occurs at the end of a syllable and is represented as a vowel sound. The c-le is circled, dividing the word into two syllables.

Example:

Decode:

Cl   c-le
s i z (z l e)
v

Encode:

s i z zle

table	jumble
cattle	dimple
cable	humble
drizzle	temple
fable	little
candle	rattle
gamble	apple
example	assemble
embezzle	finagle
bamboozle	Constantinople

7th Syllable Type: Consonant -le (C-le) Sentences

Have students practice reading sentences for automaticity. These can also be used for dictation.

1. In no time, the light drizzle became a thunderstorm.
2. The clown can juggle sixteen apples, a dish of hot noodles, and a candle.
3. The accountant liked to doodle during math class.
4. If you want to impress the noble princess, do not get her a little bauble for a gift.
5. Do not giggle while you gargle.
6. When the water has boiled, the electric kettle will turn itself off.
7. The scoutmaster's bugle is on the marble table in the foyer.
8. The proud poodle jumps over puddles to keep his paws clean.
9. Even as adults, Gertrude and Arlene still quibble over silly matters.

Have students practice reading sentences for automaticity. These can also be used for dictation.

10. Ask the teacher to provide an example of a fantastic essay.

11. Is it simple to assemble the purple table?

12. Can the player who fumbled the ball finagle the coach into allowing him to skip the huddle?

13. Do not let the salesman bamboozle you with gimmicks.

5th Syllable Type: Bossy R (BR)

BR - "ar"

The "r" controls the vowel and produces an entirely new phoneme.

Example:

Decode:

BR | Cl
c a r | p e t
v | c v

Encode:

c a r p e t

carbon	arctic
garment	darling
carpet	garner
jargon	marlin
market	parlay
pardon	varnish
Arctic	ardent
harbor	garlic
sarcasm	sarcastic
garden	artifact
garnet	compartment
harvest	marmalade
kindergarten	arsenic
carpetbagger	lethargic
charter	apartment
archer	carpenter
parsnip	

5th Syllable Type: Bossy R (BR) Sentences

Have students practice reading sentences for automaticity. These can also be used for dictation.

1. Add a dash of parsnip to the stuffing.
2. The Arctic wind made Arthur shiver.
3. Mark gave his darling wife a silver ring with a big garnet.
4. Will the candidate garner the votes he needs to defeat his opponent?
5. The farmer hopes to take a trip to Barbados to fish for marlin.
6. Arthur will varnish the dull cart so that it will shine.
7. Coach Marcus is an ardent fan of the game of darts.
8. Marlene will charter a plane for her trip to the Arctic.
9. Chop the clove of garlic and roast it with the marlin.
10. Do not use a sarcastic tone when you speak to Marlene.

5th Syllable Type: Bossy R (BR) Sentences

Have students practice reading sentences for automaticity. These can also be used for dictation.

11. Artifacts from the Arctic will be on display at the art exhibit.

12. The bandit got a trunk with a compartment to hide the artifacts that he stole from the exhibit.

13. Margo will slather marmalade on her crisp toast.

14. Arthur felt too lethargic to clean his apartment.

15. A carpenter made cabinets for Arthur's apartment.

16. Marlene became a kindergarten teacher.

5th Syllable Type: Bossy R (BR)

BR - "or"

The "r" controls the vowel and produces an entirely new phoneme.

Example:

Decode:

BR | O
t o r | s o
v | c v

Encode:

t or s o

extort	escort
torso	torment
distort	contort
export	forlorn
orbit	border
vortex	ornate
sordid	organize
cantor	formulate
mentor	tornado
fervor	Orlando
tractor	porcupine
splendor	opportune
instructor	organic
misfortune	torpedo
transistor	orthodox
confessor	orthodontist
ordeal	

5th Syllable Type: Bossy R (BR) Sentences

1. It is an ordeal for Arthur to clean his disgusting apartment.
2. The bailiff had to escort the witness from the stand.
3. The acrobat is so limber that she can twist her torso into the shape of a pretzel!
4. The rocket burst into orbit.
5. Do not torment your sister with a fork!
6. A trade embargo will put a stop to what you can import or export.
7. The monster will whimper if he gets lost in the storm.
8. The storm will cross the border in the morning.
9. Will the garnet make the silver ring too ornate?
10. If you organize your locker, you may find the pork chop that Mom gave you for lunch.
11. The shipmates had to formulate a quick escape plan in case a torpedo hit the ship.

5th Syllable Type: Bossy R (BR) Sentences

Have students practice reading sentences for automaticity. These can also be used for dictation.

12. During the tornado, the stork hid in the basement of Arthur's apartment.

13. Will the hurricane hit Orlando?

14. If you step on a porcupine, it will hurt.

15. When is the opportune moment to ask your darling to wed you?

16. The farmer sells fresh, organic corn at the market.

17. The dentist informed Jordan that he must go to an orthodontist to fix his teeth.

6th Syllable Type: Diphthongs (DT)

DT - "aw"

A diphthong is a gliding vowel. The mouth starts at one point of articulation and ends at another point.

Example:

Decode:		Encode:
Cl	DT	
j i g	s a w	j i g s aw
v c	c v	

withdraw

awful

jigsaw

hawthorn

awful

sawmill

crawfish

seesaw

rawhide

drawback

outlaw

mohawk

unlawful

outlaw

sawdust

awning

guffaw

trawler

lockjaw

Mackinaw

6th Syllable Type: Diphthong (DT) Sentences

Have students practice reading sentences for automaticity. These can also be used for dictation.

1. In shop class, the students each made a jigsaw.
2. The pup got a splinter in his paw from playing in a pile of sawdust.
3. Stand under the awning until the hail stops pounding down.
4. We must stop at the bank and withdraw cash because the shop will not take credit cards.
5. The vet insists that eating rawhide can harm a dog.
6. Thorns from a hawthorn tree are sharp.
7. The candidate's guffaw was intended to mock his opponent.
8. There was a long line to play on the seesaw.
9. It is not safe to fish from a trawler during a storm.
10. Do not focus on the drawbacks of the job.
11. Stir the heap of prawns and crawfish into the gumbo.
12. The class did not wish to sing the silly, mawkish song.
13. Will a mackinaw and a scarf protect Alexander from the Arctic wind?

6th Syllable Type: Diphthongs (DT)

DT - "au"

A diphthong is a gliding vowel. The mouth starts at one point of articulation and ends at another point.

Example:

Decode:

DT | BR

p a u p e r
v | c v

Encode:

p au p er

author

Austin

August

automat

audit

gauntlet

haunted

caustic

caucus

caustic

launder

Nassau

astronaut

autograph

autocrat

Milwaukee

authentic

autocrat

saucer

defraud

pauper

launder

applaud

auburn

caulderize

6th Syllable Type: Diphthong (DT) Sentences

1. Put the cup of hot cocoa on the saucer.
2. The pauper cannot afford to get a raincoat.
3. Arthur never launders his sheets; even
4. Arthur's dog will not sleep on the bed!
5. It is best not to use a caustic tone when speaking to an adult.
6. Applaud the actress for her excellent dramatic role.
7. The goddess has long, auburn locks and short bangs.
8. In his first dramatic role, the comic will portray a hermit who weeps nonstop.
9. Saul will ask the astronaut for his autograph.
10. Launch the astronaut into outer space.
11. The outlaw was born in Milwaukee, Wisconsin.
12. The man liked the authentic paintings in the art museum.
13. When the automatic gate got stuck, cars could not exit the parking lot.

6th Syllable Type: Diphthongs (DT)

DT - "oi"

Example:

Decode:

DT | BR

g o i | t e r

v | c v

Encode:

g oi t er

exploit

asteroid

goiter

oilskin

oilcloth

poison

tinfoil

loiter

sirloin

turmoil

ointment

tabloid

tenderloin

devoid

trapezoid

cloister

recoil

deltoid

standpoint

trapezoid

counterpoint

embroider

6th Syllable Type: Diphthong (DT) Sentences

Have students practice reading sentences for automaticity. These can also be used for dictation.

1. Mom will not even skim a tabloid while she waits in line at the supermarket.
2. Did the coach exploit the players in order to benefit himself?
3. The ointment will help stop Fido's itching.
4. Arlene is still in a state of turmoil.
5. Fresh sirloin makes the best hamburgers.
6. Marvin is content to cloister himself at home.
7. I will recoil if I see a rat, a snake, or a cockroach.
8. The acrobat has strong deltoids, which help her master handstands.
9. Parboil the prawns and grill them later.
10. The teacher told the math students to draw a trapezoid.

6th Syllable Type: Diphthong (DT) Sentences

11. In a debate, you must present a strong counterpoint to contrast your opponent's main point.

12. The seamstress will embroider a silver coin on the denim pants.

13. Felix will broil the tenderloin pork chops for dinner.

14. An asteroid orbits the sun.

6th Syllable Type: Diphthongs (DT)

DT - "oy"

A diphthong is a gliding vowel. The mouth starts at one point of articulation and ends at another point.

Example: →

Decode:

DT | DT
c o w | b o y
v | c v

Encode:

c ow b o y

enjoy

tomboy

employ

boycott

oyster

disloyal

destroy

deploy

decoy

corduroy

employment

royal

foyer

cowboy

annoy

convoy

employee

alloy

disloyal

6th Syllable Type: Diphthong (DT) Sentences

1. Floyd the cowboy trains clowns for the rodeo in Austin, Texas.
2. Dustin's temper tantrums are so loud that they annoy astronauts on Mars!
3. For the winter holidays, the staff will decorate the foyer of the hotel in rich velvet.
4. Never eat an oyster unless it is fresh.
5. The activists will boycott the fur shop.
6. The hunter will use a decoy to attract birds.
7. A convoy of jeeps transported the men to the combat zone.
8. The employee does enjoy his job at the toy shop.
9. Floyd does not enjoy shucking raw oysters.
10. Combine metallic elements to form an alloy.
11. The dauphin was disloyal to the royal king.
12. Floyd flaunts his corduroy vest; his darling embroidered a lasso onto the fabric.
13. Joy got a flamboyant gown for her date with the royal prince.

Additional Lists for Hard/Soft C and G and Y as a Vowel

Soft C	Soft G	Vowel Y
accent	tangent	fancy
success	suggest	saucy
concept	rampage	cyclone
rancid	margin	cypress
cigar	ginger	mercy
decide	urgent	cylinder
cinder	frigid	bicycle
conceal	digit	cyberspace
proceed	indulgent	gypsum
eccentric	gentle	gymnast
	germane	clergy
	impinge	allergy
	converge	urgency

Notes

Notes

Notes